Learn to Draw Manga

MANGA
MARTIAL ARTS FIGURES

Illustrated by
Richard Jones & Jorge Santillan

PowerKiDS
press
New York

Published in 2013 by The Rosen Publishing Group, Inc.
29 East 21st Street, New York, NY 10010

First Edition

Produced for Rosen by Calcium Creative Ltd
Editor: Sarah Eason
Editor for Rosen: Sara Antill
Book Design: Paul Myerscough

Illustrations by Richard Jones and Jorge Santillan

Library of Congress Cataloging-in-Publication Data

Jones, Richard.
 Manga martial arts figures / by Richard Jones & Jorge Santillan. — 1st ed.
     p. cm. — (Learn to draw manga)
 Includes index.
 ISBN 978-1-4488-7875-8 (library binding) —
 ISBN 978-1-4488-7946-5 (pbk.) — ISBN 978-1-4488-7952-6 (6-pack)
 1. Martial arts in art—Juvenile literature. 2. Comic books, strips, etc.—
Japan—Technique—Juvenile literature. 3. Cartooning—Technique—
Juvenile literature. I. Santillan, Jorge. II. Title.
 NC1764.8.M38J66 2013
 741.5'1—dc23
                                        2011053448

Manufactured in the United States of America

CPSIA Compliance Information: Batch # B4S12PK: For Further Information contact Rosen Publishing, New York, New York at 1-800-237-9932

Contents

Drawing Manga Martial Arts Figures

"Manga" is a Japanese word that means "comic." Manga characters come to life in this book of martial arts experts. Try out some moves of your own and learn to draw Manga!

Manga martial arts

In this book, we are going to show you how to draw some of the world's greatest fighting arts, Manga-style!

You will need

To create your Manga figures, you will need some equipment:

Sketchpad or paper
Try to use good quality paper from an art store.

Pencils
A set of good drawing pencils are key to creating great character drawings.

Eraser
Use this to remove any unwanted lines.

Paintbrush, paints, and pens
The final stage for all your drawings will be to add color. We have used paints to complete the Manga figures in this book. If you prefer, you could use pens.

Nunchaku Fighter

This deadly warrior is armed with a nunchaku, a Japanese weapon made of two wooden sections and a chain.

Step 1

Draw the outline for your fighter using cone shapes for the arms and legs.

Step 2

Pencil the facial features, muscle lines, and the chain of the nunchaku.

Step 3

Add the tunic, pants, and the belt. Add light shading to the folds of the clothing.

Step 4

Give your martial arts fighter a bright red outfit, with a purple belt. Add white highlights and a blue floor mat beneath him.

Ninja Attack

Ninja were fierce Japanese fighters who practiced a martial art called *ninjutsu*. They were famous for moving unseen among enemies, then making a killer strike!

Step 1

Your ninja warrior should stand with legs stretched wide and holding a sword in each hand. Draw a circle for the head and a rectangle for the body. Pencil the arms and legs.

Step 2

Draw the eyes and the mask this trained killer wears to hide his face.

Step 3

Now add detailed lines. Pencil the ninja's tunic and pants. Add the belt and hood. Your warrior should wear sandals and carry a sword sheath on his back.

Step 4

Add some light shading to the eyes to give the ninja a sinister expression.

Sharpen your skills

Ninja fought with many weapons and wore different disguises.

Step 5

Some people believe that ninja may have worn dark clothing, to help hide their movements at night. Paint your warrior with a black tunic, hood, and gloves. Use blue for his shirt and pants. Add a red outline and paint the mat beneath him brown.

Karate Kicker

Karate is an ancient Japanese martial art that features punches, elbow jabs, and high kicks.

Step 1

Draw the outline for this girl character, with one leg stretched upward and her arms to one side. Exaggerate the size of the front leg to add perspective.

Step 2

Pencil the facial features and the muscle of the front leg.

Step 3

Add lots of detail with wild, ragged hair. Shade the eyes and add the clothing and boots.

Step 4

Give this young fighter bright blue hair and blue eyes. Color the top and boots red and add a yellow belt. Her shorts and gloves can be white.

Futuristic Fighter

This Manga character has returned from the future, wielding ancient martial arts weapons!

Step 1

Draw your fighter with her back toward you and her head turning over her shoulder. Exaggerate the size of the left hand and leg so they look much larger than her head to create a sense of perspective.

Step 2

Draw the two nunchaku weapons your Manga warrior will carry.

Step 3

Now add detail. This fighter has long hair and is wearing a skirt and boots. Pencil the detail of the facial features.

Step 4

Use a very fine-tipped pencil to add lots of extra details to really bring the warrior to life. Erase any rough lines from your earlier drawings. Notice the pattern on the nunchaku, the jewel on the glove, and the folds of the skirt.

Sharpen your skills

You can change the hairstyle of your figure. Why not try one of these options?

Step 5

Give your Manga girl bright purple hair. Choose a palette of pinks, with a strong pink for the waistband and sash, and with pink ribbons for the top. Color the skirt gray and the boots brown. Choose dark gray for the glove and weapons. A brilliant gold finishes the jewelry.

Kung Fu Warrior

Kung fu is an ancient Chinese martial art in which warriors are trained to use weapons with great skill.

Step 1

Create a leaping pose for your fighter, with one leg raised in the air ready to kick out. Have him holding a wooden staff.

Step 2

Draw your character's eyes, nose, and mouth. Pencil muscles and the outline for the hair.

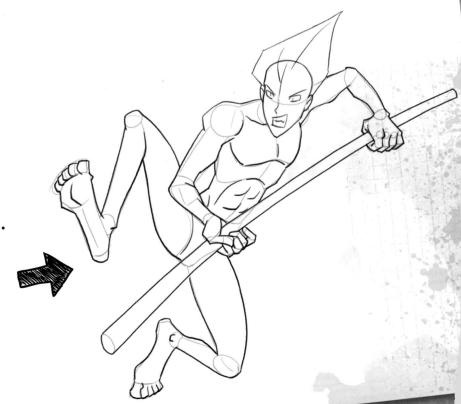

Step 3

Use a fine-tipped pencil to add very fine muscle lines, facial features, and the pants. Draw a belt and the bands of the staff.

Step 4

Paint your kung fu figure with crazy purple hair and green pants. Use purple for the belt. Paint the staff brown.

Noble Samurai

Samurai were highly trained Japanese warriors who fought and lived by strict rules.

Step 1

Create the outline for your samurai by using long cone shapes for the powerful legs and arms. Pencil a circle for the head. Draw your warrior with his back knee raised up.

Step 2

Draw the features of the face and add muscle lines to the body.

Step 3

Now add greater detail by drawing the clothing and hair. Samurai were famous for their long hair. Erase any rough lines you drew earlier.

Step 4

Pencil the sword, body armor, and eye mask. Then add lots of light shading to the figure.

Sharpen your skills

Samurai carried a long, sharp sword called a *katana*. You could give your warrior a second sword to help him in battle.

Step 5

Choose a palette of dark, dramatic colors for your samurai. Choose a gray-brown for the body armor and black for the hair and feet. Pick a gold for the knee and elbow pads, studs, and sword detail. Finish with a brilliant red for the sash and armor edging. Add some flashes of red to the gloves.

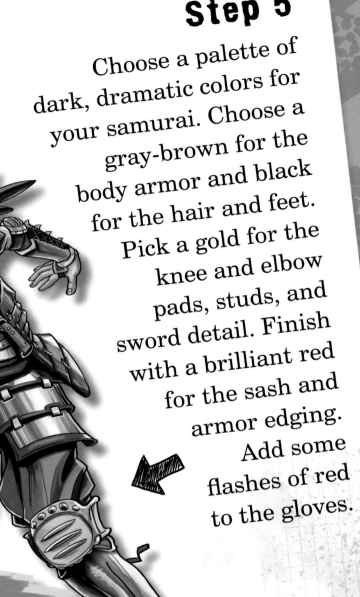

Secret Soldier

Many modern armies use martial arts as part of their soldiers' training, particularly for their special forces.

Step 1

Pencil a circle for the head of your soldier character. Her right leg should be stretching forward with her left leg bent at the knee. Have her holding her right arm foward and her left arm bent, in a defense pose.

Add the facial features and muscle lines of the body.

Step 3

Give your character a beret, boots, and a body suit. Add long hair.

Step 4

Use a fine-tipped pencil to add the detailed folds of the fabric, strands of hair, and the leg straps and belt.

Sharpen your skills

Your special forces fighter could stand in another pose, ready to attack.

Step 5

Give this expert soldier bright pink hair. Her body suit should be gray or navy, to help her move undetected in the dark. Add black boots and leg straps. Paint some white highlights on the body suit.

More Martial Arts

If you've loved drawing Manga martial arts figures, try some more!

Armed Fighter

Another futuristic fighter, armed and ready!

Tae Kwon Do Training

In tae kwon do, fighters train to deliver quick, strong kicks.

Judo Girl

This Manga fighter uses sharp punches and kicks to overcome her enemies.

Karate King

A person who practices karate is called a *karateka*.

Glossary

beret (buh-RAY) A round hat without a brim.

character (KER-ik-tur) A fictional, or made-up person. Can also mean the features that you recognize something or someone by.

deadly (DED-lee) Can kill.

detail (dih-TAYL) The smaller, finer lines that are used to add important features to a character drawing, such as eyes, ears, and hair.

erase (ih-RAYS) To remove.

exaggerate (eg-ZA-juh-rayt) Make bigger than it really is.

expression (ik-SPREH-shun) A look on someone's face that can tell you what they are thinking.

fine-tipped (fyn-TIHPD) A sharp tip of a pencil or pen.

highlights (HY-lytz) Light parts.

outline (OWT-lyn) A very simple line that provides the shape for a drawing.

palette (PA-lit) A range of colors.

perspective (per-SPEK-tiv) A sense of distance.

pose (POHZ) The way something or somebody stands.

ragged (RA-ged) Having a rough edge.

shading (SHAYD-ing) Creating lots of soft, heavy lines to add shadow and depth to a drawing.

sheath (SHEETH) A covering.

sinister (SIH-nis-ter) Threatening.

special forces (SPEH-shul FORS-es) People in the army who are specially trained for difficult missions.

staff (STAF) A wooden stick, used as a tool or a weapon.

undetected (un-dih-TEKT-ed) Not noticed by anyone.

warrior (WAR-yur) A fighter.

wielding (WEELD-ing) Holding a weapon as if about to attack.

Further Reading

Giannotta, Andrés Bernardo. *How to Draw Manga*. New York: Dover Publications, 2010.

Nishida, Masaki. *Drawing Manga Martial Arts Figures. How to Draw Manga*. New York: PowerKids Press, 2008.

Okum, David. *Manga Martial Arts: Over 50 Basic Lessons for Drawing the World's Most Popular Fighting Characters and Scenes*. Cincinnati, OH: Impact Books, 2008.

Okuma, Hidefumi. *Let's Draw Manga: Ninja and Samurai*. New York: Watson-Guptill, 2003.

Websites

Due to the changing nature of Internet links, PowerKids Press has developed an online list of websites related to the subject of this book. This site is updated regularly. Please use this link to access the list: www.powerkidslinks.com/ltdm/marts/

Index